W9-BCO-962

W is for Wrigley

The Friendly Confines Alphabet

Written by Brad Herzog and Illustrated by John Hanley

Sleeping Bear Press™

315 East Eisenhower Parkway, Suite 200
Ann Arbor, MI 48108
www.sleepingbearpress.com

© Sleeping Bear Press

Printed and bound in the United States

10 9 8 7 6 5 4 3 2 1

Library of Congress Cataloging-in-Publication Data

Herzog, Brad.
W is for Wrigley : The friendly confines alphabet / written by Brad
Herzog ; illustrated by John Hanley.
pages cm
ISBN 978-1-58536-816-7
1. Wrigley Field (Chicago, Ill.)--History--Juvenile literature. 2.
Alphabet books. I. Hanley, John, illustrator. II. Title.
GV417.W75H47 2013
796.357´640977311--dc23
2013002587

Aa

The baseball stadium located in the Lakeview neighborhood of Chicago's North Side is one of the jewels of American sports. It is bounded by four streets: Clark Street to the west, Addison Street to the south, Sheffield Avenue to the east, and Waveland Avenue to the north. Built in 1914, Wrigley Field is the oldest ballpark in the National League and one of only two major league stadiums (along with Boston's Fenway Park) to host baseball for at least 100 seasons. The Cubs have called Wrigley home since 1916, a match made in baseball heaven.

Since the ballpark's very first major league game on April 23, 1914 (between the Chicago Federals and the Kansas City Packers), fans have enjoyed the atmosphere at a place that is often called the Friendly Confines. They watch from the rooftops and bleachers and box seats. They sing "Take Me Out to the Ball Game" and "Go, Cubs, Go." They watch numbers change on the antique scoreboard and long fly balls disappear into the ivy-covered outfield walls. They cheer on their hometown heroes—Chicago legends with names like Pafko and Santo and Sandberg. And always, they root, root, root for the Cubbies.

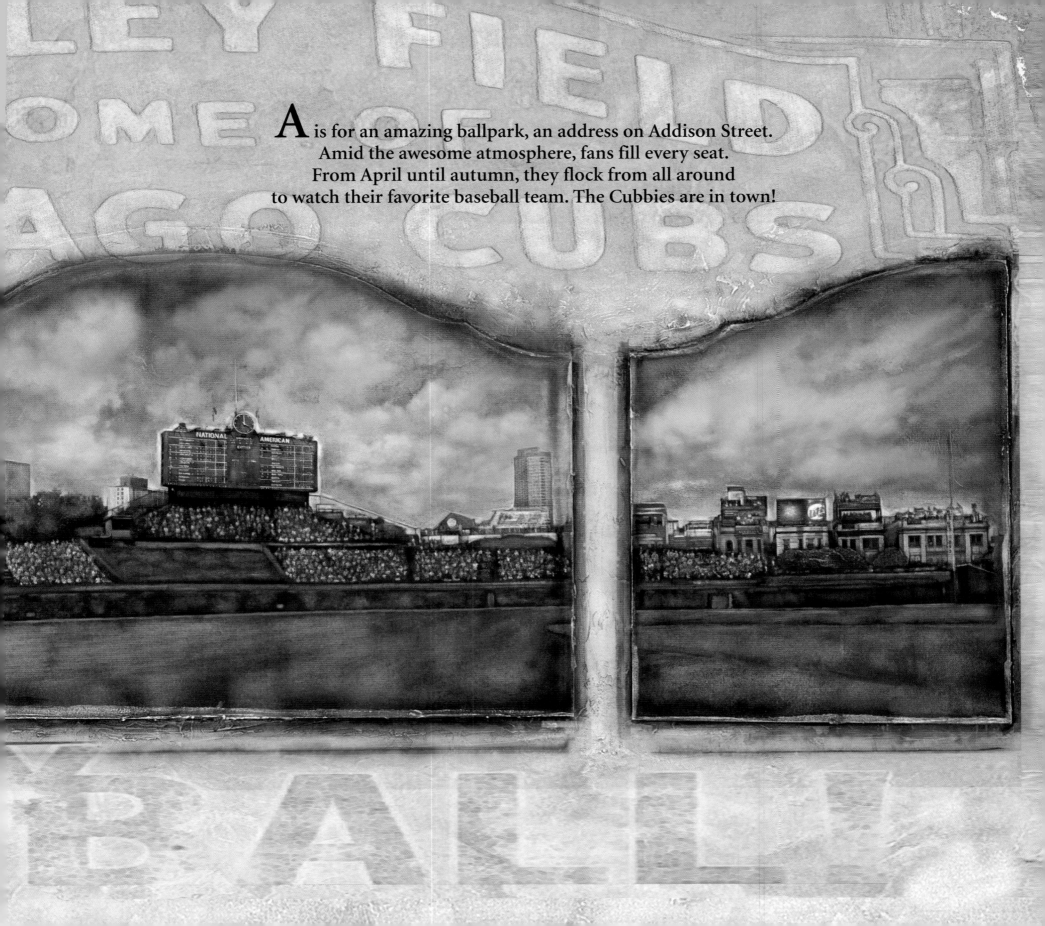

A is for an amazing ballpark, an address on Addison Street.
Amid the awesome atmosphere, fans fill every seat.
From April until autumn, they flock from all around
to watch their favorite baseball team. The Cubbies are in town!

Bb

The bleachers behind Wrigley's ivy-covered walls are perhaps the most famous seats in baseball. In 1977, a comedy stage play called *Bleacher Bums* was written by members of Chicago's Organic Theater Company. Set in the right field bleachers, the play follows a group of "Wrigley regulars" during a game against the St. Louis Cardinals on a sunny afternoon. In fact, entire books have been written about the bleacher regulars and how they have their own traditions and sense of community. One regular, Stephanie Leathers, published a newsletter called "Bleacher Banter" for 20 years. Another, Carmella Hartigan, attended hundreds of games over more than three decades after retiring from a housecleaning job in 1967. Well into her 90s, she would put on her pink Cubs cap, ride two buses to reach Wrigley and crack jokes with her friends until the final out.

B is also for bullpen, where relief pitchers warm up before entering a game. Most major league bullpens are located behind the outfield fence, but Wrigley's are situated in foul territory.

B is for the benches beyond the outfield wall,
where fans bask in the sun and have themselves a ball.
Of this beloved building's many famous features,
nothing brings as much joy as the Wrigley bleachers.

In 1906 the American League's Chicago White Sox beat the National League's Chicago Cubs 4 games to 2 in the World Series. It was the last time the crosstown rivals met during the season until 1997, when interleague play began in Major League Baseball. The Cubs beat the Sox 8–3 in the first Crosstown Classic on June 16, 1997. Now the teams meet six times each season—three games at each home stadium. The team that wins the most games each year (or the final game if it's tied 3–3) is awarded the Crosstown Cup.

Some of the best Crosstown Classic games have taken place at Wrigley Field. In 2010 both starting pitchers had no-hitters through six innings (the Cubs won 1–0, thanks to a one-hitter from pitcher Ted Lilly). In 2009 the Cubs were losing 5–1 in the bottom of the eighth inning, but they rallied to win 6–5. And during an 11–7 Cubs victory in 2008, outfielder Jim Edmonds homered twice in one inning!

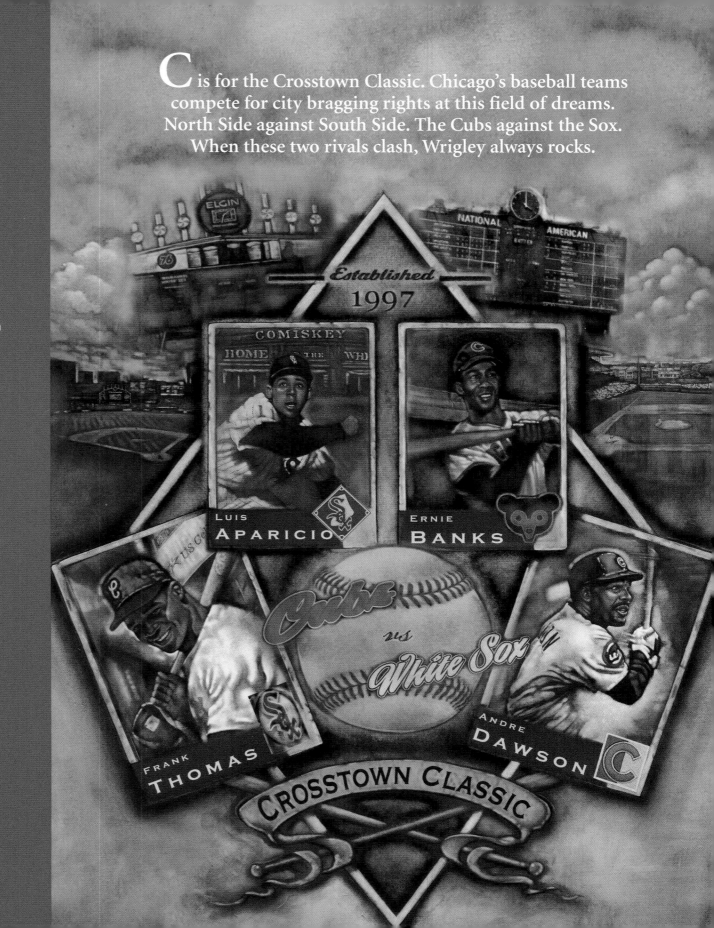

C is for the Crosstown Classic. Chicago's baseball teams compete for city bragging rights at this field of dreams. North Side against South Side. The Cubs against the Sox. When these two rivals clash, Wrigley always rocks.

Since the early 1980s, yellow numbers have been painted on Wrigley's outfield brick walls, stating the distance from home plate to that portion of the wall. It is 355 feet to the left field corner, 400 feet to the deepest part of center field, and 353 feet to the right field corner. Actually, the home run distance is just a bit shorter because a chain-link fence is mounted on top of the wall and is angled toward the outfield. During the 1969 season there were several occasions when fans interfered with fly balls or even fell onto the field. So the fence, known as "the basket," was installed in 1970. A ball that lands there is a home run. Sometimes a fan reaching for a ball lands there, too.

Long fly balls are often greatly affected by the wind at Wrigley Field. If the wind is "blowing in" from nearby Lake Michigan, it often turns would-be home runs into outs. If the wind is "blowing out" toward the lake, it can carry fly balls into the bleachers.

On Wrigley's outfield bricks, the yellow numbers dare
each batter to swing hard and hit it beyond there.
D A slugger steps up to the plate. The pitcher? He looks tense.
is for dimensions, the distance from home to fence.

E e

Wrigleyville is the nickname given to the restaurants, taverns, and apartment buildings surrounding the stadium. The focal point of the neighborhood is the corner of Clark and Addison streets, where Wrigley's famous red marquee welcomes fans to the ballpark. The marquee was installed in 1934 and was painted blue for nearly three decades before being repainted red. At night, the words "Wrigley Field: Home of Chicago Cubs" are lit in red neon. An electronic message board, which was added in 1982, announces everything from birthday wishes to scheduled events to "Cubs Win!"

In 2010 two Illinois colleges played the first football game at Wrigley in 40 years. The purple-uniformed Northwestern Wildcats were the home team against the University of Illinois, so the famous marquee was temporarily repainted purple.

The entrance to the ballpark. That's our letter E. "Home of Chicago Cubs," shouts the red marquee. Energy! Excitement! The sign provides a thrill to every eager Cubs fan and the folks in Wrigleyville.

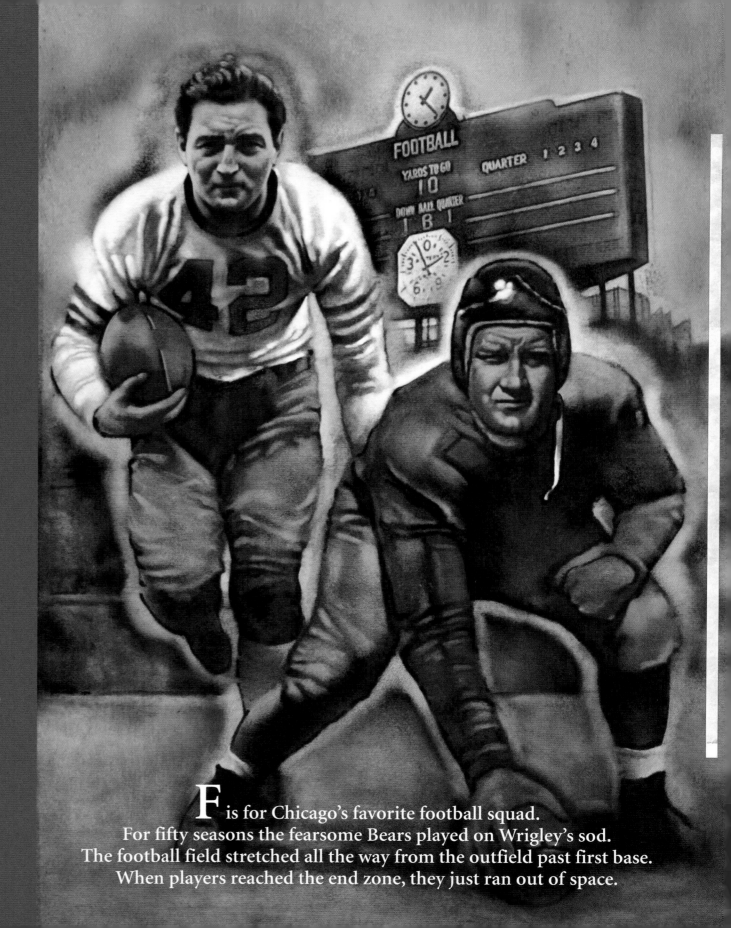

Between 1921 and 1970 Wrigley wasn't only a baseball stadium. It was also home to the National Football League's Chicago Bears. In fact, until 2003 it actually held the record for the most NFL games played in a single stadium (365 regular season games). Before moving into Wrigley, the football team was called the Decatur Staleys, but owner George Halas said, "If baseball players are Cubs, then certainly football players are Bears." The Bears won eight league championships while playing at Wrigley, but the football field was a tight fit. One corner of the south end zone was actually cut off by the visiting team's dugout!

Many other sporting events have taken place at Wrigley Field. On New Year's Day 2009, the Chicago Blackhawks and Detroit Red Wings faced off in an outdoor hockey game on the iced-over field—the NHL's annual Winter Classic. Along with rock concerts, rodeos, and circuses, the ballpark has hosted professional soccer matches, boxing and wrestling competitions, a Harlem Globetrotters exhibition, and even a snow ski–jumping event in which the skiers landed just behind second base.

F is for Chicago's favorite football squad.
For fifty seasons the fearsome Bears played on Wrigley's sod.
The football field stretched all the way from the outfield past first base.
When players reached the end zone, they just ran out of space.

Gg

Fans generally sing "Go, Cubs, Go!" after a Cubs victory. It was recorded early in the 1984 season by Chicago singer-songwriter Steve Goodman, who also wrote two more songs about his beloved Cubs. Goodman passed away at age 36 in September 1984, just four days before the Cubs clinched the National League East Division title. It was the team's first title of any kind in 39 years.

G is also for goat, as in the Curse of the Billy Goat. The Cubs' last World Series appearance came way back in 1945. The Cubs had a 2-games-to-1 lead over the Detroit Tigers in the World Series that year when local tavern owner Billy Sianis attempted to attend a game at Wrigley—with his pet billy goat, which was turned away. An angry Sianis supposedly said, "The Cubs, they ain't gonna win no more." They lost that World Series to Detroit and haven't returned. Over the years, the team and fans have playfully tried to reverse the curse by bringing goats to the ballpark and apologizing.

How do fans support the team? With 40,000 voices strong. **G**—a catchy song.
They belt out "Go, Cubs, Go," our
"Hey Chicago!" they all shout. And then, "Whaddaya say?"
"The Cubs," sing the Wrigley fans, "are going to win today."

Harry Caray (his birth name was Harry Carabina) broadcast major league games for four different teams from 1945 to 1997, including 11 seasons with the Chicago White Sox (1971–81) and his final 16 years with the Cubs. Along the way, he became one of the most beloved figures in Chicago sports history. Fans loved his oversized black glasses, his sense of humor (he liked to try to pronounce players' names backward), his trademark call of "Holy cow!" and his off-key rendition of "Take Me Out to the Ball Game." After his death in 1998, a statue of Caray was placed in front of the entrance to the Wrigley bleachers.

Caray is honored in the Cubs Walk of Fame, which consists of banners hanging from the ceiling on the main concourse at Wrigley Field. Most of the honorees are former players like Bill Buckner, Don Kessinger, and Hank Sauer. But also celebrated are longtime radio commentator Lou Boudreau, longtime clubhouse manager Yosh Kawano, and Frank "Pat" Pieper, who served as the Wrigley public address announcer for 59 years.

H h

H is for "Holy cow!" It was Harry Caray's way of cheering on the hometown heroes at the ballpark every day. This Hall of Fame announcer was a Cubs fan to the core. His heart and voice were as big as the glasses that he wore.

Ii

The ivy covering the red brick outfield walls is Wrigley's most famous feature. It was planted in 1937 by Bill Veeck, Jr., who was then the 23-year-old general manager of the team (his father was team president). In later years, Veeck would own three different American League teams—including the Chicago White Sox. Eventually, he was elected to the Baseball Hall of Fame. But in the last years of his life, he spent much of his time rooting for the Cubs from the Wrigley bleachers.

Chicago's favorite summer foliage was originally 350 bittersweet plants and 200 Boston ivy plants, but the Boston ivy soon took over. Veeck came up with the idea after visiting another ballpark—Perry Stadium in Indianapolis, Indiana—but Wrigley is currently the only professional ballpark with ivy-covered walls. Generally, the ivy begins to bloom as spring turns to summer. If a batted ball is lost in the ivy vines, the outfielder signals by raising his hands, and the batter is awarded a ground-rule double.

I is for the ivy, those famous blooming vines that grow during the summer at the Friendly Confines. Throughout the ballpark's history, many batted balls have been lost amid the greenery on those outfield walls.

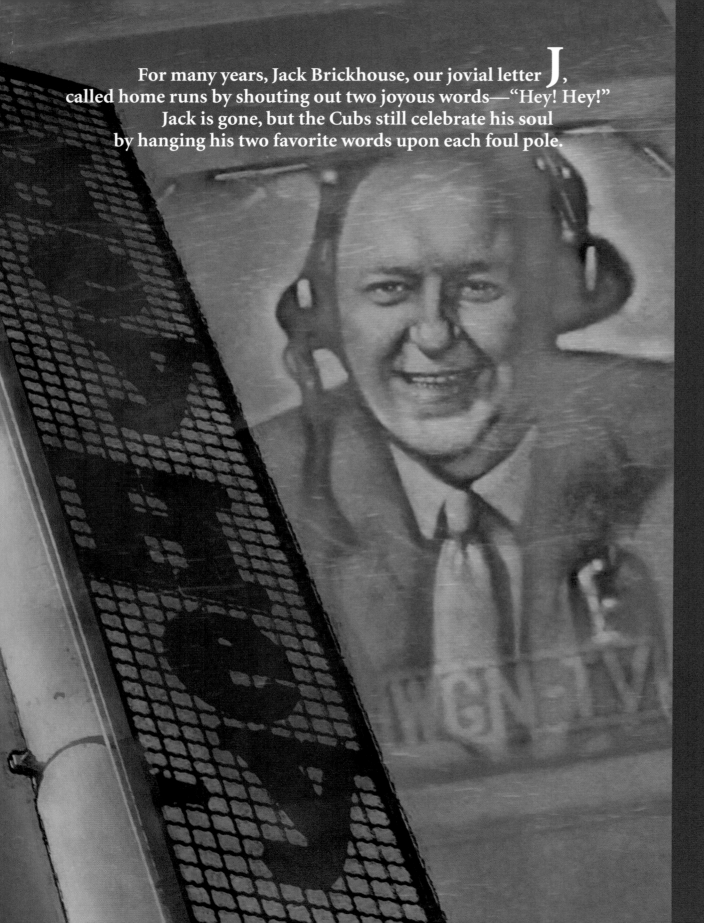

For many years, Jack Brickhouse, our jovial letter J, called home runs by shouting out two joyous words—"Hey! Hey!" Jack is gone, but the Cubs still celebrate his soul by hanging his two favorite words upon each foul pole.

J j

The words affixed to the screens on both foul poles at Wrigley are a perfect way to honor longtime play-by-play announcer Jack Brickhouse and his beloved home run call. In his remarkable career, Brickhouse covered everything from Chicago Bears games to political conventions. But he was best known as the voice of Chicago baseball for parts of five decades. He started as an announcer with radio station WGN in 1940 and then became the first face seen on WGN-TV, which has telecast Cubs games since 1948. He continued to call Cubs games until his retirement in 1981, when he was replaced by Harry Caray.

Brickhouse worked more than 5,300 baseball games during his long career. Until 1967 he handled play-by-play duties for both Chicago baseball teams because they rarely played home games at the same time. He always hoped to broadcast a World Series between the Cubs and White Sox. His wish, before there were lights at Wrigley, was: "Every game would go extra innings. The seventh and final game would be called because of darkness."

The King of **K**'s is Kerry Wood. It's amazing what he did
when he was but 20 years old, really just a kid.
He tied a big league record and even matched his age
by striking out twenty batters on the Wrigley stage.

K k

In Major League Baseball history, only two pitchers have struck out as many batters as their age. The first was Hall of Famer Bob Feller, who struck out 17 as a 17-year-old for the Cleveland Indians in 1936. The other is Kerry Wood, who achieved the feat in only his fifth appearance as a starting pitcher for the Cubs.

On May 6, 1998, against the Houston Astros, Wood delivered a dominant pitching performance. He allowed no runs, no walks, and only one hit. He struck out the first five batters he faced, and he kept going. By the time the very last batter swung and missed, it was the 20-year-old rookie's 20th strikeout, a mark equaled only by Roger Clemens (twice) and Randy Johnson in a nine-inning game. "I couldn't imagine ever doing this," Wood said afterward.

During Wood's incredible game, fans in the Wrigley bleachers held up signs adorned with the letter "K." It wasn't for Kerry. K is the symbol for strikeout on a baseball scorecard.

Many people believe that Wrigley's first night baseball game occurred in 1988, when permanent lights finally arrived. But that's not true. More than four decades earlier, the All-American Girls Professional Baseball League All-Star Game was played at Wrigley under temporary lights. But Wrigley's first major league night game was played on August 8, 1988. Ninety-one-year-old Cubs fan Harry Grossman counted down, "Three . . . two . . . one . . . Let there be lights!" He then pressed a button and six light towers flickered on above the diamond. But the game was rained out after 3½ innings. One *Chicago Tribune* writer joked, "Someone up there seems to take day baseball seriously."

One of the most dramatic moments at Wrigley occurred 50 years before the field had lights. During a late-season game on September 28, 1938, the Cubs and the first-place Pittsburgh Pirates were tied 5-5 in the ninth inning. But the overcast sky had grown so dark that the umpires decided they would cancel the game if neither team scored in the inning. With two outs in the ninth, Cubs catcher Gabby Hartnett broke the tie with a game-winning home run. The Cubs went on to win the 1938 National League pennant, and because "gloaming" is another word for twilight, Hartnett's hit was dubbed "The homer in the gloamin'."

The last of its kind for many years, Wrigley was well known
for hosting only day games. The sun, it always shone.
But now the afternoon fun extends into warm nights. L is for the lights.
Cheer loudly for a lovely evening. L is for the lights.

Ernie Banks played 19 seasons as a short-stop and first baseman at Wrigley Field. He earned the National League Most Valuable Player Award in 1958 and 1959 and was so beloved in Chicago that he was known as "Mr. Cub." Banks hit 512 home runs in his long career (290 at Wrigley), and he popularized a nickname for his favorite ballpark: the Friendly Confines. Always known for his sunny outlook, Banks loved baseball so much that he often stated that one game per day wasn't enough. When he was inducted into the Baseball Hall of Fame in 1977, he thrilled the many Cubs fans in attendance with his signature phrase: "We got the setting—sunshine, fresh air. The team is behind us. So, let's play two!" In fact, "Let's Play Two" is inscribed on the pedestal of the Ernie Banks statue located near the main entrance to Wrigley Field.

M is for a marvelous player known as Mr. Cub,
who hit mammoth home runs when he swung the club.
There was nothing in this world Ernie Banks would rather do
than play a baseball game. So he said, "Let's play two!"

Nn

N is for six numbers flying high above the park.
They honor six Cubs legends. Each man made his mark.
Among Chicago's baseball greats, nobody quite ranks
with Maddux, Sandberg, Jenkins, Williams, Santo, Banks.

The retired uniform numbers of six legendary Cubs fly on pinstriped flags atop the Wrigley foul poles. Ernie Banks (#14) was the first to have his number retired by the team, in 1982. His number flies from the left field foul pole, along with that of longtime Cubs third baseman and broadcaster Ron Santo (#10), who was finally inducted into the Baseball Hall of Fame in 2012.

Atop the right field foul pole fly the retired numbers of Billy Williams (#26) and Ryne Sandberg (#23). Williams, a left fielder, hit 392 home runs wearing a Cubs uniform between 1959 and 1974. A statue of Williams stands outside of the ballpark at the corner of Sheffield Avenue and Addison Street. Sandberg, a super second baseman, won the National League Most Valuable Player Award in 1984.

In 2009 the Cubs added #31 flags atop each foul pole. That number was worn by pitchers Ferguson Jenkins and Greg Maddux. Jenkins won the Cy Young Award as the National League's top pitcher in 1971. Maddux spent ten seasons with the Cubs, earning the 1992 Cy Young Award and recording 355 career victories.

The 2013 season marked the 100th summer that baseball has been played at Wrigley, but it is often called a "timeless" stadium. The organ music is one reason why. In 1941 the Cubs became the first major league team to add organ music to the festivities. The fans loved it, and the tradition spread to many ballparks throughout the country. In recent years, several teams have replaced organists with recorded music and sound effects. But the music heard by Cubs fans comes mostly from the nimble fingers of organist Gary Pressy, who has played at more than 2,000 home games since 1987.

O is also for outscored. On May 17, 1979, the Cubs were losing 21–7 to the Philadelphia Phillies before rallying and tying the game at 22–22. But in the 10th inning, Philadelphia's future Hall of Famer Mike Schmidt hit a home run into the Wrigley bleachers. The Phillies won 23–22. It was the highest scoring game since the very same teams played at Wrigley Field 57 years earlier. On August 25, 1922, the Cubs beat the Phillies 26–23.

The old-time tunes of an organ, that's our letter O.
A gentle baseball soundtrack became part of the show.
It's also for one hundred years—wow, since 1914!—
of baseball fans enjoying the sunny Wrigley scene.

The no-hitter is a rare feat in baseball. Fewer than 300 no-hitters have been thrown among the hundreds of thousands of games in major league history. However, on May 2, 1917, at Wrigley, two pitchers threw nine innings of no-hit baseball in the *same game*! Chicago's James "Hippo" Vaughn pitched a gem that day. Through nine innings, neither he nor Cincinnati Reds pitcher Fred Toney gave up a hit. But one of them had to lose. In the tenth inning, a Cincinnati hitter poked a soft single into right field. After a Cubs error, Jim Thorpe stepped to the plate with two men on base. This was the same Jim Thorpe who had been an All-American football player and an Olympic gold medal–winning track and field star. Thorpe swung and the ball bounced right to Vaughn, who threw it to his catcher, Art Wilson. But Wilson dropped the ball, and the run scored. Toney pitched a hitless tenth inning. The Cubs lost the game 1–0, and Vaughn was the losing pitcher in a game both men deserved to win.

P p

P is for a pitching pair. They were nearly perfect for one day.
The year was 1917. It was the second day of May.
The crowd was on its feet. Who would dare to sit?
For nine innings, neither pitcher allowed a single hit.

VAUGHN

TONEY

After a game, a white flag with a blue "W" flying above the center field flagpole signifies a Cubs win. If a blue flag with a white "L" is raised, that means the Cubs lost. For many decades, the color schemes were reversed—a blue flag for victory, and a white flag for defeat. But it was pointed out that a white flag often means, "I surrender!" And the Cubs never give up. Some fans even bring white "W" flags with them—to home and away games—in anticipation of a Cubs win.

On April 24, 2008, an extra white flag could be seen flying atop the Wrigley scoreboard. Instead of letters, there were blue numbers on it —"10,000," celebrating the team's 10,000th win on the road the previous night. Dating back to the start of the National League in 1876, the Cubs hold the record for the most wins by a team in a single city.

Q is for a question. Who won the game today?
How can you find out? At Wrigley there's a way.
When the Cubs pull out a win, that's always a cue
to raise a crisp, white flag with a big blue "W."

Q q

R r

$\mathbf{R}$ is for the rooftops along two avenues,
a treat for diehard Cubs fans. What amazing views!
Sit high above the ballpark, beyond the outfield green.
Soak up the sun. Have some fun. Enjoy the baseball scene.

Several residential buildings near Wrigley are even older than the ballpark. Because the buildings have flat roofs, fans have long watched games from way up there, sitting either above Waveland Avenue (beyond left field) or Sheffield Avenue (beyond right field). Before the 1980s, a small number of fans would sit in lawn chairs and watch the game for free. But now tickets are sold (in partnership with the team) to the 16 buildings with rooftop views. Some rooftops have bleachers that hold up to 200 people and serve restaurant-quality food.

On one rooftop along Sheffield Avenue, known as the Lakeview Baseball Club, the bleacher seats are located above two famous signs. One reads *Eamus Catuli*, which is Latin for "Let's Go, Whelps" (the nearest translation of "Cubs"). The other is a series of letters and numbers that changes each year, for example "AC0467104." The "AC" means *Anno Catuli* or "In the Year of the Cubs." The numbers mark the years that have passed since the team's last division championship (04), their last World Series appearance (67) and their last World Series win (104).

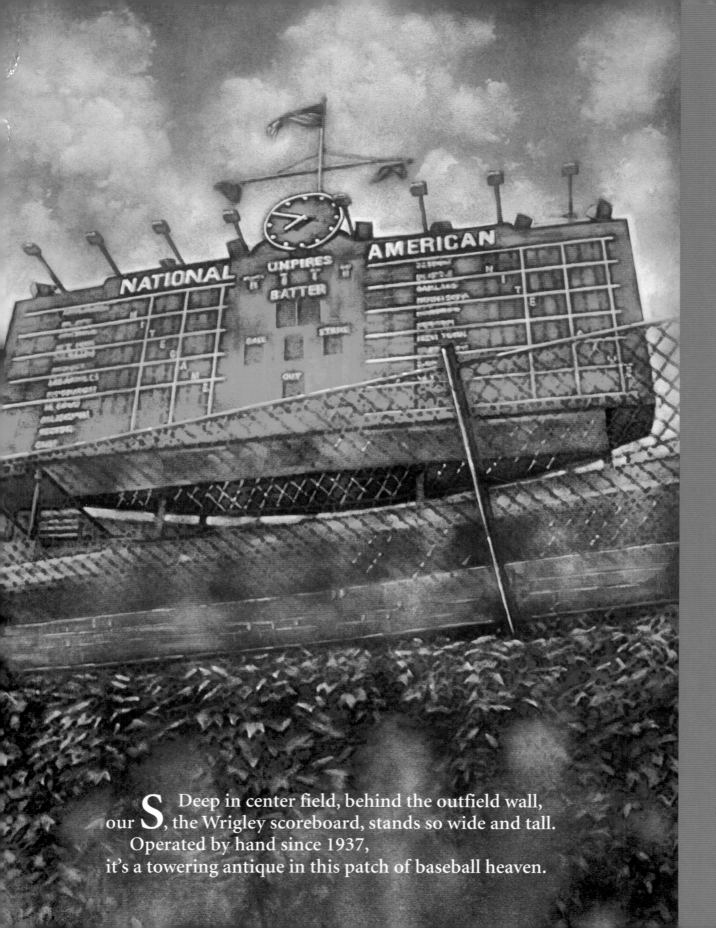

Most Major League Baseball stadiums utilize completely electronic scoreboards. But not Wrigley. Wrigley's famous board has loomed over the center field bleachers since it was constructed out of sheet steel in 1937. For more than seven decades it has been operated by hand. A number turner updates the score of the Cubs game and other baseball games by replacing the numbers from within. Just about the only thing that has changed dramatically about the scoreboard (besides the clock placed atop it in 1941) is the color. The green board was originally reddish-brown, a color that can still be seen by the number turner inside it.

The 27-foot-tall, 75-foot-wide scoreboard is located so deep in center field that no batted ball has ever hit it, although sluggers like Roberto Clemente and Sammy Sosa have come close. Another S, professional golfer "Slammin' Sammy" Snead, actually did hit it, but he used a golf club. Before the game on Opening Day in 1951, Snead placed a golf ball on a tee at home plate and then bounced it off the scoreboard. He then hit a ball *over* the scoreboard. "Yeah," said Cincinnati Reds manager Luke Sewell, "but can he hit a curveball?"

S Deep in center field, behind the outfield wall,
our S, the Wrigley scoreboard, stands so wide and tall.
Operated by hand since 1937,
it's a towering antique in this patch of baseball heaven.

S s

There's a Wrigley Field tradition during the seventh inning.
We root, root, root for the Cubs, whether or not they're winning.
"Take Me Out to the Ball Game," a tradition, our letter T.
"All right! Lemme hear ya! Ah-one, ah-two, ah-three . . ."

T t

Jack Norworth, the man who wrote the lyrics to "Take Me Out to the Ball Game," had never attended a baseball game. But the man most identified with the song, announcer Harry Caray, saw thousands of them. For 16 years, during the seventh-inning stretch at Wrigley (and before that at Comiskey Park), fans would wait to hear the song's opening chords played on an organ, followed by Caray's familiar voice. The whole stadium would sing with him. In the middle of the song, he would change the lyrics slightly to "root, root, root for the Cubbies."

Caray passed away in 1998, but the tradition continues at Wrigley Field. The team invites local and national celebrities—athletes, actors, singers, politicians—to lead the fans as guest conductors. Most try to begin the song the way Caray always did: "All right! Lemme hear ya! Ah-one, ah-two, ah-three . . ."

Two other baseball traditions were popularized at Wrigley: keeping foul balls and throwing home run balls back onto the field. Of course, Cubs fans only throw the ball back if it was hit by someone on the opposing team.

Workers began adding a second deck to the Wrigley grandstand—an upper deck—after the 1926 season. Although it was only half finished in 1927, the team still became the first National League team ever to draw more than one million fans in one season. The upper deck was completed before the following season began.

Nearly two dozen flags fly high atop Wrigley's upper-deck roofs. Some are red, some white, some blue. All honor special events in Cubs history. The flags above the left field roof commemorate the years in which the Cubs have played in the post-season, including their ten World Series appearances. Above the right field roof, eight flags honor various feats. For instance, one flag has "HAWK" on one side and "8" on the other, in honor of 1987 National League Most Valuable Player Andre "Hawk" Dawson, who wore number 8. Another says "HACK" and "191" —for Hack Wilson's record achievement of 191 runs batted in during the 1930 season.

U u

U is Wrigley's upper deck, a view from high above.
Surrounded by fellow fans, it's the Cubs we love.
It's also for an umpire. That's him way down below.
Safe at home in Wrigley Field, we all enjoy the show.

Wrigley was the nation's first ballpark to have permanent concession stands, and vendors have been roaming the aisles for decades. In fact, Bill Veeck, Jr., the man who directed the planting of the famous ivy along the ballpark's outfield walls, started his career as a young popcorn vendor at Wrigley.

One of the most remarkable vendors ever to roam Wrigley was a man named Dan Ferrone. He began as a 24-year-old, selling soda. On his first day on the job, in 1938, he made $2, which wasn't bad considering that a bottle of soda cost ten cents. Ferrone spent three decades as a postal employee and another 11 years working at a bank, still vending in his spare time. In 1981 he became a full-time vendor, and he didn't stop selling his wares—including peanuts and programs—at Wrigley until he retired at age 81 in 1995. Ferrone sometimes said he hoped to be the first vendor ever elected to the Baseball Hall of Fame.

V v

V is for the vendors wading through the Wrigley crowd,
vying for attention, their voices booming loud.
"Peanuts! Popcorn! Cracker Jack!" they shout above the din.
Everything tastes better when the Cubbies win.

The ballpark wasn't always known as Wrigley Field, and it wasn't always home to the Cubs. The home team for the ballpark's first game was the Chicago Federals (or Chi-Feds), who played in an organization called the Federal League. Team owner Charlie Weeghman called his new stadium Weeghman Park. On Opening Day, April 23, 1914, the Chi-Feds beat the Kansas City Packers 9–1. The next year the team was renamed the Chicago Whales in a fan "pick-the-name" contest, and the team won the league championship.

After the 1915 season, when the Federal League went out of business, Weeghman became part owner of a new team: the National League's Chicago Cubs. He moved them from their wooden ballpark on Chicago's West Side to his steel-and-concrete stadium on the North Side. On April 20, 1916, the Cubs beat the Cincinnati Reds 7–6 in 11 innings in their first game there.

By 1920 the Cubs had a new owner, William Wrigley, Jr., who ran a large chewing gum company. He changed the stadium's name to Cubs Park, but six years later it was renamed once more. It would forever be known as Wrigley Field.

W
W
W

A man named Charlie Weeghman owned the Chicago Whales
and built the wondrous ballpark that tells so many tales.
He and William Wrigley, Jr. soon moved the Cubs in there.
Without them, there'd be no Wrigley Field. So that's our W pair.

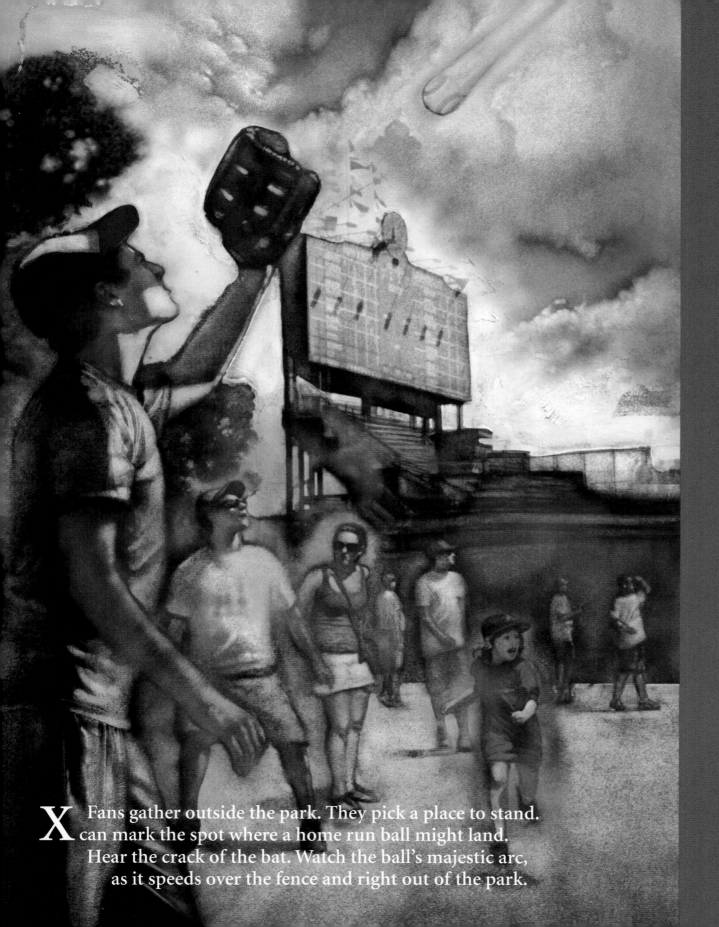

During batting practice, and even during games, many fans gather on Waveland Avenue (behind left field) and on Sheffield Avenue (behind right field). Often these are gangs of kids—"ballhawks"— wearing baseball gloves and waiting eagerly. Their goal is to catch a home run ball.

Former Cubs slugger Dave "King Kong" Kingman hit perhaps the longest home run ever at Wrigley. He did it on a very windy day when he played for the New York Mets. On April 14, 1976, Kingman launched the ball out over Waveland Avenue. The ballhawks turned and started running down a perpendicular street, Kenmore Avenue. They watched as the ball struck a porch three houses away. The hit has been estimated at more than 530 feet from home plate.

On May 11, 2000, Cubs slugger Glenallen Hill hit a home run that also flew far over the left field fence and over Waveland Avenue. But this one landed on one of the famous Wrigleyville rooftops. "I have never seen that!" shouted announcer Chip Caray, grandson of legendary Harry Caray. "On top of the building!"

X Fans gather outside the park. They pick a place to stand. can mark the spot where a home run ball might land. Hear the crack of the bat. Watch the ball's majestic arc, as it speeds over the fence and right out of the park.

On October 1, 1932, during Game 3 of the World Series between the Yankees and the Cubs, Babe Ruth and his opponents were talking trash to each other. In the fifth inning, Ruth batted against pitcher Charlie Root. With two strikes against him, he pointed two fingers ... somewhere. Cubs players later insisted he was pointing at their bench, telling them there were only two strikes. Ruth later claimed he pointed to the center field bleachers. On the next pitch, he hit a home run to deep center field. Did he call his shot? Nobody knows for sure, but it certainly is a big swing and a myth.

Few people know that the great Lou Gehrig followed Ruth to bat that day, hitting a home run on the very next pitch. But it wasn't his first visit to the stadium. Twelve years earlier, when his high school team competed in the inter-city championship at what was then known as Cubs Park, the 17-year-old Gehrig hit a mammoth ninth-inning grand slam.

Y is for a Yankees star—the Sultan of Swat.
Legend has it that one day Babe Ruth "called his shot."
He pointed toward the Wrigley bleachers, then that's where he hit it.
But nobody knows for sure if he really did it.

Yy

Zz

Zachary Taylor Davis

Four years before he designed the ballpark that would become known as Wrigley Field, architect Zachary Taylor Davis crafted blue-prints for Comiskey Park, where the Chicago White Sox played from 1910 through 1990. Constructed at a cost of $500,000, Comiskey was called "the world's greatest baseball palace." Although Wrigley cost only half as much to build in 1914, it is the only one of the two still standing.

Construction began on February 23, 1914, only two months before the opening home game, but workers labored feverishly and finished the stadium with three days to spare. Wrigley has been renovated several times over the years. In fact, in the spring of 2013 Cubs owners unveiled a plan for a $500 million renovation that included cre-ation of an enormous video screen beyond the outfield. But the stadium still retains the basic "jewel box" design conceived by Davis so many years ago.

Z is also for zero world championships at Wrigley. The Cubs won their last World Series title in 1908, the longest champion-ship drought of any major North American team. But the ballpark is almost always filled to near capacity—more than 41,000 seats—and Cubs fans remain unfailingly loyal. Every April, hope has a box seat.

CHICAGO WHALES BASEBALL CLUB

Coordinates
41 56 '54"N
87 39" 20" W
Surface
Grass
Construction Cost
$250,000

First Game

April 23, 1914

Z is for Zachary Taylor Davis. It was in this architect's mind
that Wrigley Field was first created. The park was his design.
Thinking of the fans, he drew the perfect place for them.
Even a century later, the diamond's still a gem.

WEEGHMAN PARK

19 **FEDS** 14
CHICAGO BASEBALL CLUB